**Date: 3/7/17**

# WINDMILLS

Charlotte Hunter

rourkeeducationalmedia.com

## Teaching Focus:

Have students find capital letters and punctuation in a sentence. Ask students to explain the purpose for using them in a sentence.

## Before Reading:

### Building Academic Vocabulary and Background Knowledge

Before reading a book, it is important to set the stage for your child or student by using pre-reading strategies. This will help them develop their vocabulary, increase their reading comprehension, and make connections across the curriculum.

1. *Read the title and look at the cover. Let's make predictions about what this book will be about.*
2. *Take a picture walk by talking about the pictures/photographs in the book. Implant the vocabulary as you take the picture walk. Be sure to talk about the text features such as headings, the Table of Contents, glossary, bolded words, captions, charts/diagrams, or index.*
3. *Have students read the first page of text with you then have students read the remaining text.*
4. *Strategy Talk – use to assist students while reading.*
   - *Get your mouth ready*
   - *Look at the picture*
   - *Think…does it make sense*
   - *Think…does it look right*
   - *Think…does it sound right*
   - *Chunk it – by looking for a part you know*
5. *Read it again.*
6. *After reading the book, complete the activities below.*

### Content Area Vocabulary
*Use glossary words in a sentence.*

clockwise
conductor
converts
electricity
electrons
shaft

## After Reading:

### Comprehension and Extension Activity

After reading the book, work on the following questions with your child or students in order to check their level of reading comprehension and content mastery.

1. *How is the electricity floating windmills produce sent to land? (Summarize)*
2. *Why is wind energy better for our planet? (Asking questions)*
3. *How is the speed and direction of the wind checked? (Text to self connection)*
4. *What do a windmill and an airplane have in common? (Summarize)*

### Extension Activity

Make your own windmill! You will need paper, scissors, glue stick, pencil with eraser, and a push pin. Cut two identical squares from the paper. Glue the sides of the squares together. Apply glue not just along the edges, but on the entire back area of the squares. Cut the square halfway to the center. Gather the four corners toward the center without creasing the paper. Glue the ends in place or just hold them together with your hand. Insert a push pin at the center. If you did not glue the ends of the paper, the push pin should hold all four ends together. Wiggle the push pin around to make the hole a bit larger. Push the pin onto a pencil's eraser. Don't push on too tight to allow the pinwheel to spin more freely. Finally, try blowing at the edges of the pinwheel to make it spin. Loosen the pin a bit if the blades do not rotate well. Enjoy!

# TABLE OF CONTENTS

# WIND POWER

Have you ever held a pinwheel and watched it turn in the breeze? The wind spins the pinwheel just like it spins the blades of a windmill.

Windmills use the power of wind to create **electricity**.

Windmills are also called wind turbines. The power they create is considered renewable energy, because there is always wind on Earth.

# CLEAN ENERGY

Wind energy is clean energy, because it does not require burning coal and it does not produce pollution.

Wind energy is thought to be a healthier choice for people and the planet.

Windmills have been used since the Middle Ages. They were originally designed to use the power of the wind to mill, or grind, grain into flour.

# HOW IT WORKS

Most windmills have three blades that spin **clockwise**, like an airplane propeller. The hub of the windmill is the central part attached to the blades.

Some windmills can be up to 650 feet (198 meters) tall, when you include the blades. They are the largest rotating structures in the world.

Each blade is usually between 115 and 148 feet (35 and 45 meters) long. The blades and the hub together are called the rotor.

blade

hub

blade

blade

Wind turbine blades spin because of lift. This is the same force that allows airplanes to fly. If the blades are facing the same direction, they will spin.

Computers check the speed and direction of the wind using instruments at the top of the windmill.

wind instruments

The computers make sure the hub of the windmill is always turned so that the blades are facing the wind.

wind

When the wind turns the blades, it slowly spins a large **shaft** inside a turbine.

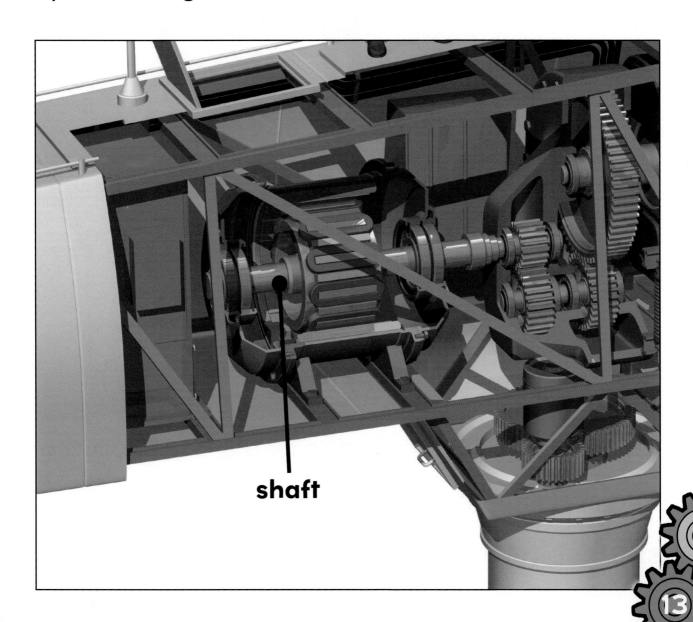

shaft

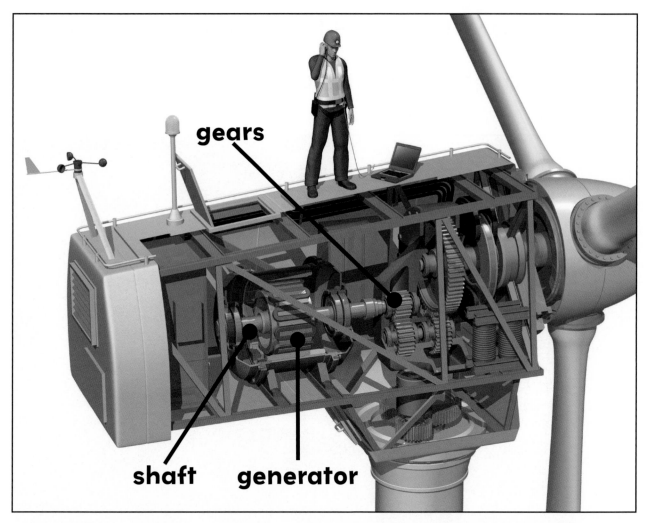

gears

shaft  generator

This shaft is connected to gears that connect to a smaller shaft, which turns faster. This shaft spins a generator.

A generator is a device that moves **electrons** through a **conductor** to make electric power. A generator uses a magnet that forces electrons to move along a wire while putting pressure on them.

# POWER UP!

The generator **converts** the mechanical energy from the rotation of the windmill's blades into electrical energy.

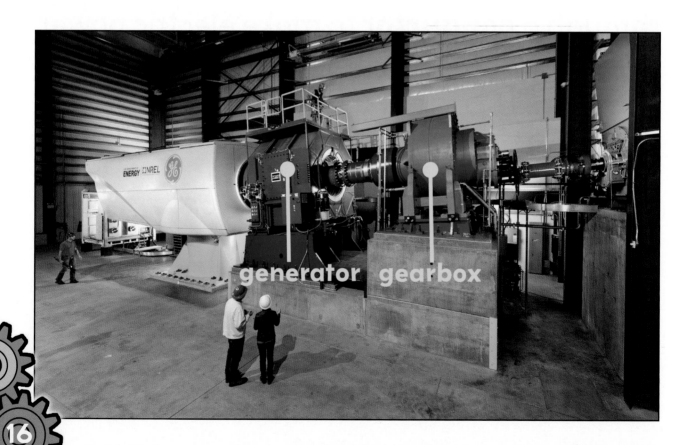

generator   gearbox

Mechanical energy is the energy an object has because of its motion or position. Electrical energy is made by the flow of electric charges through a conductor.

Windmills aren't just found on land. They can also be installed on floating structures in the ocean. The electricity from floating windmills is sent to land through underwater cables.

The electricity created by the windmill is sent through transmission lines to a power company's substation.

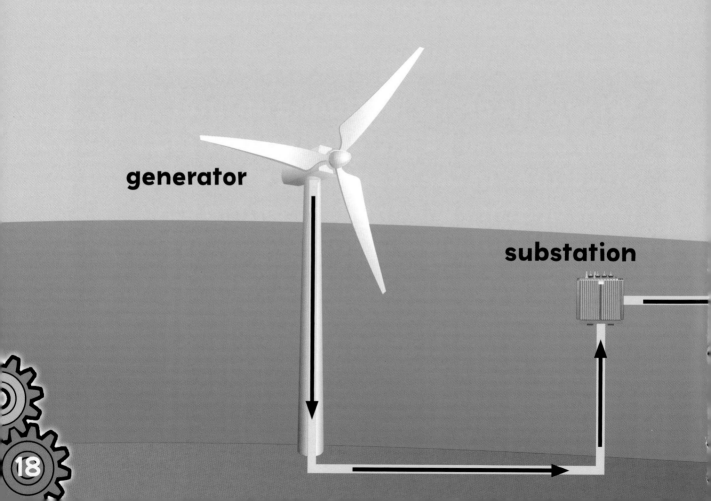

generator

substation

From there, the electricity is sent to homes, businesses, and schools.

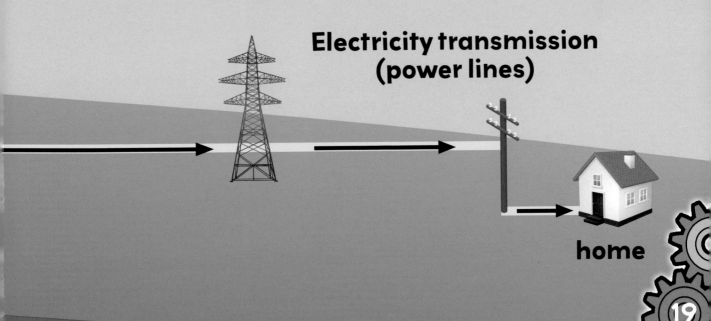

**Electricity transmission (power lines)**

**home**

The amount of electricity a windmill produces depends on the diameter of the rotor and the speed of the wind.

rotor diameter

Some windmills generate enough electricity to power a small town!

# PHOTO GLOSSARY

 **clockwise** (KLAHK-wize): The direction a clock's hands move is called clockwise. Objects that rotate or spin in this direction are said to move clockwise.

 **conductor** (kuhn-DUHK-tur): A conductor is a substance that allows heat, electricity, or sound to travel through it.

 **converts** (kuhn-VURTS): When something converts, it changes into something else.

 **electricity** (i-lek-TRIS-i-tee): Electrical power that is created and distributed through wires to power homes, businesses, and schools is called electricity.

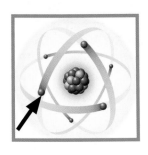 **electrons** (i-LEK-trahns): Electrons are tiny particles that move around the nucleus of an atom. They carry a negative electrical charge.

 **shaft** (shaft): A shaft is a rotating rod that transmits power in a machine or engine.

# INDEX

## WEBSITES TO VISIT

www.ducksters.com/science/environment/wind_power.php

www.eschooltoday.com/energy/renewable-energy/wind-energy.html

http://energy.gov/eere/wind/how-do-wind-turbines-work

## ABOUT THE AUTHOR

Charlotte Hunter is a writer who loves learning about technology and the amazing people who design things to make life easier for everyone.

**Meet The Author!**
www.meetREMauthors.com

PHOTO CREDITS: Cover © LL28; Title Page © studiocasper; Page 4 © Hongqi Zhang; Page 5 © Inaki Antonana Plaza; Page 6 © Richard Gillard; Page 9 © Joe Gough; Page 10 © Kelvin Wakefield; Page 11 © pennablanca; Page 12 © esemelwe; Page 13, 14 © cornishman; Page 16 © Dennis Schroeder/NREL; Page 20 © Andrea Vitting; Page 21 © BanksPhoto

Edited by: Keli Sipperley
Cover and interior design by: Jen Thomas

**Library of Congress PCN Data**

Windmills / Charlotte Hunter
(How It Works)
ISBN 978-1-68191-688-0 (hard cover)(alk. paper)
ISBN 978-1-68191-789-4 (soft cover)
ISBN 978-1-68191-888-4 (e-Book)
Library of Congress Control Number: 2016932565

Printed in the United States of America, North Mankato, Minnesota

**Also Available as:**